A Collection of Poems

A Journey Through Life

by

Cheryl Williams

DORRANCE
PUBLISHING CO
EST. 1920
PITTSBURGH, PENNSYLVANIA 15238

Dorrance Publishing Co
585 Alpha Drive
Suite 103
Pittsburgh, PA 15238
Visit our website at *www.dorrancebookstore.com*

ISBN: 978-1-4809-5607-0
eISBN: 978-1-4809-5584-4

Shades of Gray

Life isn't always black and white
Though some see it that way
Some eyes are blind and can't define
The many shades of gray

Each one unique in its own way
And it's designed for you
Be proud and never be afraid
To live your shade of gray

Familiar colors are embraced
While unfamiliar shunned
Accentuate your shade of gray
And live your life your way

A vision-impaired colored world
May minimize your worth
But never, ever change your way
Live your shade of gray

Distractions

Never blur your journey
With the smoke of
One man's hate

Never let the man who fails
Distract you from your fate

Don't let the avid lazy mind
Tell you that you can't try

Never trust an injured man
To lead your inner mind

A poisonous heart
Can't see his path

So he will block your view
Trying to distract you
From things you need to do

So focus on the task at hand
Ignore his envious schemes
Don't succumb to
His wild demands
Of trivial lunacies

The Way Home

Burnt with life's woes, she struggles down
this deserted road all alone...
The stressors of life overwhelm her soul

Regrets of past mistakes, torment, and terrorizing pain
tear-filled eyes swollen with lasting effect of shame
blue blood of despair boils in her veins

Caught up in this depressive mode
blinded, on a road filled with woes
Not knowing that every trial is not a curse,
and good things often fall apart, allowing better
things to unfold, and even though at times
life might seem cold

The hardships and disappointments in life
have set her up for a path of hope
Her eyes open to her purpose, her goals
Now she can see her destiny clearly

As she struggles down that deserted road,
She beholds the beauty of the flower and the
struggles it endures to grow, sprouting
through compacted concrete stones
Showing her a path to walk
Helping her find the way home

A Fragile Mind

A broken mind, subconsciously intertwined with
the rippling effects of the ever-changing tide
Carried to and fro, with no direction or place to go

Consumed with the unpredictability of a world
filled with greed and poverty, man against man
Polluted minds of corruption, infesting our land

Battling the demons of hatred and strife, engaged
in endless wars, resulting in suffering and anguish,
pain and sorrow, no hope for a chance at tomorrow

What shall we do with these broken, fragile minds?

How can we change the raging tide, penetrate the
insides, replacing the constant negative, with hope,
peace, and happiness, riding on the winds of a new
perspective, changing the tides, embracing the positive

Positive Energy

A combusted world of loss and sadness
Defused with kindness and laughter

Hatred spreading on life's lawn
Like stubborn dandelions

Encounters the weed killer
Of love and compassion

When anguishing pain seems eternal
Comforting arms proves immortal
Life's revolving doors of uncertainty
Meets an unfettering escape of positivity

When naked negativity pursues you
Surround yourself with life's blanket
Of positive energy

Phenomenal

You may see me struggle
As I lie awake
You may see my anger
But you will never
See me break

The rivers I cross are many
Banks gaping, water tall
The rocks are hard and slippery
Yet I will never fall

When life squirts bitter lemons
To sour my sweet day
Regardless of how bitter
I won't succumb to pain

With perseverance I walk on
Resilience my backbone
With faith I'll make it
Through the storm
I am phenomenal

The Void

I am blind!
My eyes buried deep inside
the abyss of this shallow,
absent mind
Incomprehensible darkness
Devoid of colorful lines

Where am I
How did I get here
Let me see
Who's out there

The fearful dread of the unseen
Terrorizes me
Imprisoned by the haunting
walls of faded memory

Maneuvering aimlessly between
the blurred lines of aphantasia

Trapped in an unknown world
cold and unfamiliar...

Hero

When life's problems
Seem bigger and tougher
Than you
Your attitude will determine
If you will get through

When obstacles consume,
and intimidate you
Your commitment is needed
To get you through

When you are terrified,
bewildered, and
discouraged with life
Don't ever give up
Keep your eyes on the prize

Whatever curveball
Life throws at you
Keep pressing forward
Find the hero in you

Envelop

Callused feet toughened by
a world of constant pressure

Hurting eyes strain in an attempt
to pull it all together

An exhausted heart racing on empty
searching for serenity

Speechless with no words left to say
The constant revolving doors of life
has left her that way

Lost in a puzzling maze, with no way out,
of this never-ending situation
She ran to the ocean in desperation

In its calm and beauty the ocean
showed her mercy,
opening its mouth
swallowing up her pain

Enveloping her soul in a cleansing wave
The peace only its healing waters can bring

A Beautiful Mind

A reticent man engrossed
in regretful memories
Dissipating idiosyncrasies

Willpower versus reluctancy
Opposing reflections concurrently
enveloping a restless soul

Simultaneous spiritual warfares
Battles between good and bad
Unleashed within the inner man

The incessant battlefield
of overwhelming flames
Seizing the human brain

Eternal bliss still inwardly exists
The omnipresence of the divine
Encapsulating the innermost being

Emotionally conflicting thoughts
Choices between right and wrong
Wrestling deep inside
A beautiful mind

Pilgrimage

A subconscious mind
On a soul-searching journey
That human eyes can't perceive

The distance of unpredictability
Deprived a compass as a guide
A sojourner on an obscured ride

Faced with obstacles and doubts
Sharp twists and zigzag turns
Clouding the way out

Resounding light of hope and refection
lightens every rocky path
With courage and determination

Trees of resilience drinking life
From waters of tireless patience
Through astounding faith-filled eyes

A spiritual pilgrimage
The journey of a lifetime
Beyond the heavenly skies

Where Is Home?

Face down in the dirt
Breathless
The place I'm from,
buried deep in the ground
The ashes of burnt memory
Choke me
I suffocate swallowed up by
the hollow space, without escape

Tell me it's okay a while to stay
For I have lost my way
My soul bleeds, heart grieves
Endless darkness surrounds me
Buried in the earth beneath

Bare feet, chasing shadows that lure me,
into the broken pieces of history
I am lost, the past evades me
Sanity escapes me
Please let me go
I don't live here no more

Running to and fro, needing hope
Help me find the way home
Show me the path to a new destination
Arm me with the strength and vigor
A mind enlightened by a higher power

The Dreamer

He was a small man
In a big city
Fighting for a dream
One he couldn't see

At times his hope
An all-time high
Other times hope
Waved goodbye

He worked so hard
For many years
But no one
Ever seemed to care

Most nights he burned
The midnight oil
Now the tables
Have been turned

Investing his whole life
It seemed
His time, his money,
His self-esteem

It all just couldn't
end this way
There must be
a better way

Just when he thought
it was too late
A light appeared
As the dawn breaks

Darkness fades
As sunlight streams
He must wake up
And live his dreams

Music

I feel the sensual energy
Devouring up the notes

Such curative medicine
To my aching soul

Music is my therapy
My healing remedy

A self-prescribed prescription
That fills me sensually

The rhythm overpowers
Body and soul alike

The aroma intoxicates me
As my passion comes alive

Optimism

At times we're faced with challenges
That seem too much to bear

No matter how tough the road gets
There's always someone there

So look a little closer
See the one that he's sent you

The universe is listening
It will take care of you

So don't become discouraged
This hopelessness shall pass

Life is still worth living
Regardless of our past

A Turning Point

Struggling down a deserted road of life
A fear-filled journey riddled with twists and turns
stress and heartaches of impending storms
Nerves unearth with regrets of past wrongs
eyes swollen, minds entrapped in a zone
A depressive mode... with no way out
No relief from the hurt and doubt
The pain, the aching brain sustains
Falling through the cracks, tattered, bruised,
and scratched, left exposed, with infected,
decaying wounds that hurt
Tormented and torn, at a point of no return
Blinded by the stressors of this world
In the midst of it all, she beholds the beauty,
the sun peeking through the clouds
Among the chaos and confusion
A glimmer of hope, a feeling of knowing that no
matter how rugged the road gets, there is
always a light at the end of the stretch

Serenity

Enriching lives
Improving health
Rejuvenating minds

Tranquility the key
To eternal bliss
The universe
Working in unison
Creating happiness

A higher power
A supernatural force
Designating the future
Of our universe

Empower thy soul
With the medicine
Of positive thinking

An attitude of thankfulness
Changes the outcome of
Life's hopes and direction
Bringing us to a destination
Of peace of mind and positivity
Freedom from a world of worry

Loss

The darkness hovers over me
A sudden sense of loss
The emptiness torments me
Thoughts flooding back and forth

The memory of the endless love
The blessed love we shared
Stood there in silence, frozen
Heartbroken with despair

Thinking of that blessed day
That seems so far away
When we will be together
In a special kind of way

Entrapped

It was the last night
a night like no other
the life I once knew
was certainly over
My hurting brain
going insane, left in
the dark in a room
with no frame
Trapped in my nightmare
a road with no end
in-depth conversations
play on in my head
Thoughts of what could be
remain never said
voices continually replay
in my head
Pain overwhelms me
wherever I go
From corner to corner
In this wall-less home

Shine

Never allow the darkness
To swallow you up
Shine your luminous light

Don't allow the vastness
To perpetuate your fears
Shine your luminous light

Never, ever let circumstances
Destroy your faith
Shine your luminous light

Don't let rejection
Opinions or opposition
Dim your luminous light

Green-Eyed Monster

He is a restless soul
Never focusing
Completely
On his own goals

Wherever he roams
He loathes
Those living their dreams

Comparing himself to all
The other monsters
In his community

Never appreciating
His own ability

Anger and hatred
Blinded him

Soon his eyes couldn't
Hide the disdain he felt

They became green
With jealousy

A raging monster
Filled with envy

The Silence

Tears streaming down her face
A flicker of light shone through
Only for a fleeting moment
Leaving as quickly as the dew

Today is another
One of those days
The endless darkness
With no end game

Days morphed
Into nights with no
Differentiating line
Of the vanishing time
The absence of hope
With relentless pain
Lacking authority
To end this tirade

The cold, hard rocks
Serve as a pillow
Life dragged her
Down so low

The rocks are
Her comates
If it wasn't for the rocks
She would go insane

Empathy

Don't confuse me
with my brother

He feels for you
I care for you
He recognizes your pain
And shows concern for you

I understand your shame
And walk in your shoe

When your heart breaks
I am right here beside you

When you feel hopeless
I stretch a hand out to you

I identify with your loss
And relate to your concerns

I don't recognize your struggles
As sympathy would

I connect with your hardships
As empathy could

Crossroads

Standing at the crossroads
With no sense of perception

Watching as the cars go by
Each one a different direction

A mindset of perplexity
With no end in sight

The struggles of my inner man
Has dimmed my guiding light

The emptiness engulfs me
Blinded by my confused mind

Faced with such uncertainties
Down this path that we call life

A Blessing

When life dumps its issues on you
And situations seem unbearable
Meditate on the blessings

When the aches and pains
Wash away hope like the rain
Contemplate on the blessings

When problems seem insurmountable
And disappointments deem unconquerable
Focus on the blessings

When blinding snow prevails
Feeling trapped with no escape
When tyranny reigns
And all else fails

Never forget that
Life is still a blessing

The Majestic Ocean

Eyes intrigued by
The amazing beauty
Of the horizon
As the sun slowly faded
Into the distance

Standing on the shore
In utter amazement
Looking out at the offing
Admiring the dolphins
And the glistening waters

Inspired and empowered
In awe of the majestic ocean

The Unknown

Eyes swollen shut
Heart on her sleeve
Fingers latched on tight
Muscles quiver in disbelief

Crestfallen by the plight
That life can end this way
One moment all seems bright and gay
The next he's passed away

You can't predict what may befall
With matters of the heart
Life corners can turn quickly
And throw you off its path

So cherish every moment
Big, medium, and small
Before death's pain and sadness
Come knocking at your door

The Hidden Treasure

The evening sun slowly drifted behind the clouds
As a multicolored ray of light descended from above

Albert sat quietly on his front porch rummaging through
An old shoebox of priceless treasures

While many were oblivious of the letter-writing era
He was blessed to have that beautiful piece of her

Caressing every folded piece of paper with loving care
Indulging in the magical words her lips once conveyed

Dating back to nineteen-fifty-nine, words breathing life
Rolling off his tongue with such beauty and delight

Heartbroken as her silent words lifted off the page
Sobering tears escaping eyes filled with hurt and pain

Reminiscing on the intoxicating aroma
Fragrance of lavender, her delicate persona

Sitting there unaware of the darkness amidst
As twilight slowly faded with heavenly bliss

Every word his aching soul devoured
Was the sweet breath of his beloved

Hypocrisy

My fellow human
I see your dark side
And I see your light

I see the way you
conceal your flaws
By covering them up
with your warmth
You hide amongst
the branches of the trees
Like a chameleon changing
colors ever so quickly
Yet I see

You avoid the brightness
of the sun
Yet your shadow reveals
what you don't want found

I am perplexed and dismayed
How you smile at me
then treat me with such disdain

You offend and ignore me
Without realizing that I can see
Not every smile mends a broken heart
Not every spoken word comes from the heart

I see your hypocrisy and insincerity
Your devious and deceitful ways
Your heart contradicts the words of your lips
But the universe will always have the final say

Fear Cripples Dreams

She stood there frozen
Knees clanging
like cymbals in a
marching band

Feeling lost,
vulnerable, scared
A hopeless soul
In a distant land

Heart racing
Palms sweating
Knees knocking
Teeth clattering

She knew
she couldn't
pull it off

Trepidation sunk in
The vicious enemy
Of courage

Silence thickening
Moments crumbling
Voices whispering
Time ticking

What was she thinking
Were they right all along?

Aura

You are beautiful, my love
Just the way you are
Your magnificent lissome stature
Transcends above the clouds
Tender, slender loving arms
Embrace your robust soul
It's mesmerizing witnessing
The inner you unfold

Your smile lights up the night skies
Like a swarm of fireflies
Your heart explodes with kindness
Like burning dynamite

The aura of your presence
Brings creatures far and near
Heavenly incense emanates
Their broken hearts repair

A Web of Deceit

My heart is gone, emotions I feel none…
I am numb, from the trauma you inflicted
on me, entrapped in your web of deceit,
your tendrils you attached tightly
sucking the life out of me slowly….
My pores sweat drops of blood, as I desperately
tried to save you…when your shallow heart
gave out…

I was there for you when you hurt, helping
you heal your wound…there when you lost
your home, supporting you with an income

I treated you like a sister, risking my life,
my sanity, traveling in the pouring rain just
to check in on you…

And this is how you repay me?

Your heart is a cesspool full of stinking lies
Your conscience has shriveled up and died
You said you loved me a million times, but
it was just an expression of your guile

You assured me that you had my back
Yet you stabbed me…plunging the knife
through the wall of my ribcage…
ripping my heart out of my chest, leaving me
bleeding through a gaping hole filled with regrets

With dishonesty and false pretense you spun a
cunning web of deceit, intricately you weaved
like the black widow, you pulled me in with a smile
Covering my eyes, injecting your venomous vile

My mind encaged...trapped in this charade
The same questions replay in my
head again and again…

How could I have fallen for this
Staring blindly into the abyss,
reflecting, contemplating, internalizing…
Why…why was I so blind...
Your treachery escaped me…I was too naive to see

I trusted you...yet you betrayed me
My gullible mind couldn't perceive…
your vicious scheme...

Yet my strength I regained, in my darkest hour
realizing that everything in life happens for a reason
helping me to become a wiser, more resilient human being

Emerging

Obliterate the hardships,
struggles, and pain
that stem from
a garden of
rejection and fear

Ameliorate the outcomes
with life-changing choices
Staunch work ethics
Attaining success

Graduate to mastery
Knowledge is power
Wisdom achieved
An earnest endeavor

Contemplate on the vastness
of grandeur and fame
derived from experience,
resilience, and faith

Eradicate sparseness
doubtful thoughts diminished
Emerging with confidence
Achieving greatness

The Human Eye

Narrowed eyes, only define
preconceived, flawed designs

True beauty never seen by sight,
but deep inside an open heart and mind
A beautiful plant that blossoms into
different shapes and colors of its own,
is rejected by the human eyes
appearing different from the norm

The limited human vision
confined to discrimination
Discarding the ones that don't meet the eyes
while embracing the acceptable ones

Love is blind when projected from the eyes
accepting only what is pleasing,
only those of its kind

If beauty's defining attributes were left up to
the discretion of the narrowed mind,
the beautiful truth that exists between
me and you would be hidden

Between the Lines

Fixated on a fascinating world above
Admiring the artistry of the magnificent evening clouds
Vividly coming to life between the lines

Eyes exploring beauty, the existence of colorful love
Painted so perfectly, an illustrious image of splendor
Transforming the brilliance of grandeur between the lines

Intrigued by the glorious heavenly hue, fingers transcribe
the enchanting view, tantalized by the amazing fiery skies
Transmitting powerful energy between the lines

Captivated by the appealing radiance, twilight's vigor
empowering my world, elevating me to new worlds on high
Transferring my innermost feelings between the lines

Ecstasy explodes, connecting souls to an enchanting universe
A spiritual epiphany of translucent picturesque harmony
Eyes enticed, mesmerized
Elation emerging between the lines

My hungry soul indulges in the birds-eye view, enthralled in awe,
gazing upon the glorious skies, my heart's desire satisfied
Transcribing so freely
Engrossed as I write, between the lines

Perplexed

Eyes opened wide, as I gazed up at
the heavenly skies in wonderment
Thinking out loud
Is the sky really blue
what infuses the snow with the
whiteness of cotton
and words of wisdom inspire you
What makes the wind blow
the moon glow
and thoughts in hand we hold
Where lives the conscience
the notion, of good and bad
and memory lags
How does the ocean with no
arms wave at us
and hearts filled with blood
Love and trust
I stand in awe…
Perplexed…
Do you know?

Direction

When you feel like you have lost your way
When confusion seems to be the norm of the day

When the direction of the wind you can't detect
The weathervane of life will lead and direct your steps

You must remain focused and never lose sight
Of the many reasons why you are alive

Though hardships and disappointments may abound
And a smile you replaced with a frown

Look for the glimmer of hope in the darkness
Even when the nights seem cold and hopeless

When you feel like you have lost your way
Focus on the direction of life's weathervane

Besiege

The claws of negativity
Snatches the soul
Stealing your joy

Your happiness
Leaving you
Emotionally unclothed

Eschew undue stress
Envelop your soul
In a circle of positivity

A Broken Heart

Lying wide awake
Eyes turned inside out
peering into the darkness
inside me, retrieving my
exhausted heart in a
desperate attempt
to escape the emptiness
Anguished, torn apart
Broken into a million pieces
Hopeless blood spills
She's gone, leaving a fragile
heart to bleed in an empty
hollow cavity
Deprived of oxygenated
blood, separated from true
love, dying slowly, drowning
in the sea of pain and agony
Envisioning the gentle touch
The warmth of sweet love
A glimmer of hope to hold on to

Magnificence

As I rise with the sweet
Songs of the birds
The warmth of the sun

The alluring, magnificent sunrise
Embracing the beauty of creation
My praises are sung

As I stand I raise my hands
Up to the heavenly skies
Lifting praises to the one on high

I am grateful to be alive
My purpose is to be
An ever-shining light

Across this magnificent sky
Illuminating the darkness
Where shadows once existed

Intertwining this world
In a transcending circle
Of love and happiness

Turmoil

Regrets torment the spirit
Hate crushes and destroys

Worry changes nothing
But robs a heart of joy

Anger destroys a mind at peace
Frustration strangles hope

Disappointment leaves a heavy heart
Guilt terrorizes and provokes

Expectations birth dismay
Procrastination delays goals

Vengeance burns mind's clarity
Negativity drains the soul

Farewell

Slamming the door on negativity
Closing the book on redundancy
Turning off the faucet of endless drama
Leaving the cluttered room filled with
gossip and small-mindedness
Exiting the bus bound for
destruction and feud
Raising my hand to the sky
Waving goodbye
Bidding farewell to those on the ground
Boarding a heavenly plane
En route to a peaceful destination in the sun

Equilibrium

The quest to obtain sanity
Through highways of the mind

With equalizing feelings
Of emotions running high

Balance is the driving force
Down the crazy road of life

A breakthrough on life's pathway
Mixed feelings compromised

Petals of perfect harmony
through equipoise derived

As body, mind, and soul align
Restoring peace of mind

You

You worry and fret
Yet in your haste forget
that you are truly blessed

A unique soul in a lost world
where the norm is to become
a clone of another person

Failing to accept the truth of
your amazing human assets

You must love the unique you
Embrace your strengths,
your weaknesses

Appreciate the skin you're in
You are here for a reason

There has never been
And will never be
Another you...

The Survivor

A resilient tough skin
The masterpiece of an
ingenious work of creation

Covering copious veins
Conveying the vital essence
of strength and determination
To a stoic heart

An immensely diverse human
Living through a fiery hell on earth
Possessing the nonporous skin of survival

Elucidating the severity of torture
unleashed from intense suffering
Earnestly conversing with the trees

Struggling through the woods' immense heat
Parched bare skin, bruised and battered
covered with the shade from the weeping willow

Filled with empathy the leaves whispered
as the murmuring trees divulged
Revealing the way out, the way to freedom
Defying the laws of rejection and pain
Triumphantly emerging with beauty and grace

Mary's Garden

Mary loves the landscape; it's perfection like fine art
Always admiring her neighbor's beautiful front yard
White daffodils, sunflowers, and carnations bloom
Appeasing her senses, as great joy fills her heart

When fear and darkness bring sadness and gloom
Nature's magical enchantment lightens her mood
She calls it her garden, a sweet garden of her own
A charming place to relish, the birds' soulful tunes

Spring's scintillating blossoms with fragrance so bold
An array of delicate flowers, magnificently clothed
The splendiferous trees, her aging eyes still see
A delightful fair garden that soothes her aching soul
Indulging in the satiety, nature's brilliance and beauty
Solace her soulmate, ingenuity her astounding glory
Every morning breathes hope, for a brand-new start
The all-powerful deity of nature's abundant bounty

Hope after the Rain

Believing there is a reason
for everything life brings
Searching for a way out
of a world of emptiness...
Changing one's perspective,
replacing doubt with faith
Allowing the mind to attain,
what remains after pain
Beholding the immense glory,
as a colorful rainbow appears
A sign of hope and beauty,
after the rain

Twilight's Heavenly Dew

Your illustrious, beautiful, heavenly mist,
evoking a hungry, passionate kiss

Arousing my sensual, desirous soul,
Overwhelming sensations, spontaneity exposed

Mesmerized by your stimulating fiery glow
My body and soul, with intense pleasure explode

An indulging, exhilarating, explosive love,
your magnificent beauty encapsulating my world,

A soul becoming one, with the heavens above
Captivating mind, spies through fascinating eyes,

Unable to define, the artistry and magnificence of
your glorious, majestic design

Hypnotized by the awe-inspiring twilight dew,
an expression of eternal love, between me and you

Human

You look me in the eye
Yet forget that I'm alive

I feel
Just like you do
My emotions run through veins
As yours do

You push me, mistreat me
Yet you don't see me
In your eyes I am invisible

Hear me
My soliloquy
As I release the burden
you inflicted on me

I feel anger, pain, and sadness
As you do

So why can't you see
That I'm alive
Just like you!

Do you forget
I'm human, too?

A Caring Heart

He crossed her path
for a reason
Giving her an opportunity

To make a difference
in the life of another person

Paying close attention as her
train pulled into the station

Eyes fixated and positioned
She didn't want to lose sight of him

She was convinced he needed her and
was determined to make a difference

Even if it meant missing her train
Even if it meant being late

Set in Time

Injected thoughts deposited behind,
intoxicating eyes, engrossed, in
a spellbound, mesmerizing world of souls

Captivating, sensual music,
penetrating virgin ears, caressing
the sculpted body of a god
A work of fine art

A seduction-filled fascination,
in admiration of the bulging lines
Encapsulated in a facet of overwhelming pleasure,
Fiery filled feelings, contemplated in reaction
to interactions of an exceptional creative force, of
true fineness, crafted in all the right places

A masterpiece of creation, frozen in a blanket
of mysteriously passionate recollection
A sense of belonging, absorbed in erstwhile
Reflective eyes projecting the immense cravings
portrayed by a hungry mind
Set in the vision of a past time

Treasured Love

No one compares to you, my love
Peas in a pod, like turtledoves
On cloudy days you are my sun
A forever love to treasure

The storms of life might knock us down
With windy days our love holds strong
Once prayer prevails we can't go wrong
A forever love to treasure
Rough bumps may knock us to the ground
Yet strength of wills revolves around
Warmth of the sunny sea of love
A forever love to treasure

My dearest love, you give me hope
Courage and strength for me to cope
Each part of you my heart adores
A forever love to treasure

The Campfire

The sound of children cheerfully echoing
The charming sounds of the old folksongs
Enticing aroma of marshmallows roasting
The cool night air refreshing souls
Enjoying a home away from home
A beautiful enchanted woods painted
with the foliage of the succulent bountiful bosky
Tents stretched out as far as the eyes can see
Howling fades in the distance while
laughter saturates the dense night air
Trees swaying with the gentle breeze
revealing the magnificent glow of the full moon
reflecting on the lake
Young lovers wrapped up in each other's arms
sweet love in the air, evoking desirous
pleasure, a daring, alluring atmosphere
A night of enchanting moments
building memories beneath the majestic trees
Man becoming one with nature
Around a hearty campfire

Altered Ego

An audaciously jovial demeanor
Uncontrollable spontaneous
echoes of contagious laughter
Delivered purposely with vigor
Encompassing a dense
foggy space

Improvised comical lines
satisfying eager minds
Dynamic applause escalating
Explosively energizing impulses

Vibrations of rustling sounds
Sheer enthusiasm emerging
from an audible crowd

Executing facetious, eloquent lines
An ingenious, clever mind
Hiding behind a powerhouse
of sarcastic humor

Her Song

Perched way up high, she sits there on a limb
With the rising sun as sweet morning breaks
A pleasant joyful bliss, to hear her sing
The beautiful sounds the canary makes

A blessed gift, she will always treasure
A bright ray of hope, when life seems hopeless
Exciting her heart, her morning pleasure
Such soothing tones, music pure and flawless

Each brand-new morning with the rising sun
She hopes and prays that her song she will hear
Right on time, with the sun, her friend will come
She sings her lovely song, then disappears

Uplifting heavenly, pellucid sound
To her empty soul, such fulfillment found

Healing Waters

Tranquil mood, preludes a
daunting journey of a lifetime
Rise and fall of the tides,
caressing clouds at times

Obscuring the light on the horizon
A never-ending pursuit
Staying afloat, heading for
a coast of deliverance and hope

A refreshing body of water,
thalassic, hungry waves
swallowed up my soul
immersed in the depths of purity

Spiritual healing, infusing
through veins of a life
so frail
energy restored
A new life bestowed

Captivated

A gentle breeze brushed
against my face, caressing
my warm cheeks, as I meandered
along the endearing riverbank

Mesmerized by the conspicuous,
magical, nebulous sky
Magnificently designed
Embracing the water's edge
An alluring, sensuous sight

The mystical sounds surround
Nature's musical flavors
intrinsically transmitting an array
of captivating euphony
A stroke of serendipity

Inhaling the pleasurable odor
Of the sweet evening air
The intoxicating aroma
of the sassafras and maple
A delightful fragrance of
sweet birch and cedar

The flirtatious touch of the
raindrops stroking my face
Evoking a sensation of seduction
to my quivering upper lip
Stimulating the arousal of the senses

Perfectly intertwined
Exploring the illustrious beauty
A fascinating journey
Profoundly divine...

Nature

Nature's splendor in all its glory, portraying the
awe-inspiring artwork of an all-powerful creator,
who cleverly carved the majestic mountains, covering
them with a beautiful assortment of trees and shrubs

The glorious warmth of the sun reflecting on the
splendid mountaintops, harmoniously adorned,
each complementing the other, sitting side by side
Accentuating the enchantingly colorful skies
Appeasing the naked eyes, a fascinating sight

Silent streams and bountiful rivers tightly tucked,
painted snugly between the lustrous, vibrant trees
The spectacular landscape, uplifting the spirit
stimulating and inspiring the desirous mind's eye

Captivatingly serene, tranquil piece of heavenly realm
Her stimulating fingers caressing the canvas of her soul,
Creating a masterpiece of the breathtaking beauty of nature
Walking in the artistic footsteps of her creator

A Rainbow

Bright
Colorful lights
A divine sign
Of hope and happiness
A life of celestial bliss
After the uncertainty that hid amidst
An iridescent array of healing, heavenly lights
The halo of purposeful calm satisfies the eyes
A glimpse of eternal beauty, existing beyond the skies

Life's Journey

Consumed by anger, frustrations, and hurt
Approaching the infamous crossroads of life
saturated with bends and curves

Filled with unpredictably suffocating
Undeniably overwhelming, complexities
Ignorant of the surprises the dawn might bring

Though the journey of life is flexuous
We must never let the fear of the unknown
Possess us to run and hide
Succumbing to its demise

Capturing and paralyzing our body and mind
Denying us the amazing opportunity
To fully live our lives

Life's bends and curves aren't meant to destroy
But to challenge, motivate, and elevate us
to the amazingly successful human
We were all created to become